Published by

Joshua Tree Publishing
• Chicago •

JoshuaTreePublishing.com

13-Digit ISBN: 978-1-941049-51-8

Disclaimer:

This book is designed to be included, and their presence is not an endorsement of the food items within. The opinions and information expressed in this book are those of the author, not the publisher. Every effort has been made to make this book as complete and as accurate as possible. However, there may be mistakes both typographical and in content. Therefore, this text should be used only as a general guide and not as the ultimate source of information. The author and publisher of this book shall have neither liability nor responsibility to any person or entity with respect to any loss or damage caused or alleged to be caused directly or indirectly by the information contained in this book.

Printed in the United States of America

1

2

3

4

Table of Contents

Soup, Salad & Sides

"You must never be fearful about what you are doing when it is right"
Rosa Parks

2-3 serves Cauliflower Poppers

Ingredients

1/2 head	Cauliflower, cut into florets
2 cp	Panko bread crumbs
2	Eggs, whisked
	Salt and pepper, to taste

Sauce

2 tbs	Sweet chili sauce
2 tsp	Hot sauce
1/2 cp	Plain greek yogurt
1 tbs	Honey

Instructions

1 Preheat oven to 400°

2 Dip cauliflower pieces in egg and then roll in panko until fully coated and place on a baking sheet lined with parchment paper

3 Repeat until cauliflower is coated

4 Bake for 20 minutes or until coating is dark brown and crunchy

5 While cauliflower is cooking, make sauce

6 Add all ingredients into a small bowl and whisk until smooth

7 Drizzle over finished cauliflower, reserving additional for dipping

"Girls, if boys say something that isn't funny,
you don't have to laugh"
Amy Pohler

4 serves Sweet and Sour Carrots

Ingredients

1	Red onion, chopped
3 tbs	Butter
3 lbs	Carrots
3 tbs	Honey
3tbs	Apple cider vinegar
1/4 cp	Craisins
	Capers

Instructions

1 Mix water and carrots in a skillet over medium-high; bring to a boil

2 Reduce heat and simmer, partially covered, 6 minutes

3 Increase heat to medium-high; cook, uncovered, 4 minutes or until liquid evaporates

4 Add the onion and let simmer for 2 to 3 minutes

5 Mix honey and vinegar in small bowl and add to the carrots along with butter, craisins and capers

"To be successful a woman has to be much better at her job than a man"
Golda Meir

6 serves | Al's Cornbread

Ingredients

2 cp	Corn meal		2	Eggs
1/2 cp	Self-rising flour		2 tbs	Oil
1/2 cp	Sugar		1/2 tsp	Baking soda
1 tsp	Salt			
1 1/2 cp	Powdered milk			
3 cp	Water, boiling			
2 tsp	Baking powder			

Instructions

1 Preheat oven 380°

In a mixing bowl:

2 2 cups corn meal

3 1/2 cup self-rising flour

4 1/2 cup sugar

5 1 teaspoon salt

6 1 1/2 cup powdered milk

7 Boil 3 cups water, add to mixture

Add:

8 2 tablespoons of oil, until oil disapears

9 1/2 teaspoon baking soda, stir until badder puffs

10 2 beaten eggs

11 2 rounded teaspoons baking powder

Mix Well

12 Pour into greased skillet

13 Bake 32 minutes

"We all require and want respect, men or women, black or white. It's our basic human right."
Aretha Franklin

2-3 serves Panzanella Salad

Ingredients

2 cp	Field greens
	Italian bread
1	Grape tomatoes, handful
	Orange bell pepper, sliced
	Capers, drained of liquid
1	Cucumber, chopped
1	Basil, small bunch
4 oz	Red onion, sliced
	Mozzarella balls

Balsamic Vingeraette

1 tbs	Balsamic vinegar
1 tsp	Dijon mustard
1/2 tsp	Honey
3/4 tsp	Salt
1/4 tsp	Pepper
1/4 cp	Vegetable oil

Instructions

1. Cut the cucumber, tomatoes, pepper, onion and mozzarella balls
2. Chop the basil
3. Cut the bread into cubes
4. Heat a pan over medium/ low heat and add a tbsp oil
5. Add the cubes and season with salt
6. Cook, stirring occasionally until toasted about 10 minutes
7. Combine all of the ingredients in a bowl including the capers
8. Shake dressing well
9. Add vinaigrette and toss

"You know what, bitches get stuff done"
Tina Fey

4-6 serves Green Bean Casserole

Ingredients

1 lb	Green beans, rinsed and halved
2 tbs	Butter
2 tbs	Salt
8 oz	Mushrooms, sliced into halves
1/2 tsp	Pepper
2	Garlic cloves, minced
2 tbs	Flour
3/4 cp	Vegetable broth
1 1/4 cp	Half and half
	Fried onions, cover the top

Instructions

1   Over medium-high heat, melt the butter in a large oven proof skillet

2   Add the mushrooms, 2 teaspoon salt, and the pepper

3   Cook, stirring occasionally, until the mushrooms begin to give off some of their moisture, about 5 minutes

4   Add the garlic, stir, and cook for another 2 minutes

5   Sprinkle the flour on top and stir until combined. The flour will soak up all the moisture.

6   Add the vegetable broth and simmer for 3 minutes

7   Decrease the heat to medium-low and add the half-and-half

8   Stirring occasionally, cook until the mixture is thick, 10 minutes

9   Remove from the heat and add 1/4 of the fried onions and all of the green beans

10 Give it a nice stir, combining the sauce and beans

11 Top with remaining onions and bake, about 10-15 minutes

"Most men I know rely on women to do all the literal dirty work"
Elizabeth Banks

4 serves Garlic Brussels Sprouts

Ingredients

2 lbs	Brussels sprouts
2	Garlic cloves, minced
1/4 cp	Olive oil
1 tsp	Lemon zest, grated
	Salt and pepper, to taste
1/2 cp	Lemon juice, dash
	Parsley

Instructions

1. Preheat oven 420°
2. Mix brussel sprouts in a bowl with olive oil, salt and pepper
3. Pour them on a sheet pan and roast for 35-40 minutes
4. They should be crisp on the outside and tender on the outside
5. Sprinkle with chopped parsley
6. Add 1 tablespoon each lemon juice and grated lemon zest

"As women, we must stand up for ourselves...for each other...for justice for all"
Michelle Obama

2 serves Farro Beet Salad

Ingredients

1 cp	Farro
3 cp	Water or vegetable stock
1 pk	Baby beets, 8 oz
5 oz	Chèvre goat cheese
	Balsamic glaze, to taste

Instructions

1 Cook one cup farro in 3 cups either water or vegetable broth

2 Let the farro cool

3 Place in fridge

4 Mix in cut up beets, goat cheese and add the balsamic glaze

"It's our job as women who have been given a certain amount of success and visibility to pull other women along with us"
Lena Dunham

2-3 serves Zucchini Boats

Ingredients

1 lb	Zucchini		1 cp	Cherry tomatoes, halved
1/2	Yellow onion, minced			Salt and pepper, to taste
1 tbs	Butter			
1	Egg, beaten			
3 tbs	Panko breadcrumbs			
3 tbs	Feta			
2 tbs	Parmesan cheese, grated			

Instructions

1. Preheat oven to 375°
2. Cut each zucchini lengthwise then scoop out the center pulp (reserve the pulp as will be used in the filling)
3. In a small skillet, melt the butter then add the onion and zucchini pulp
4. Cook the vegetables for about 3-5 minutes until softened
5. Add the garlic and cook for about 2 more minute
6. Add cherry tomatoes
7. Remove from heat and mix in the feta and breadcrumbs
8. Add salt and pepper to taste
9. Add the beaten egg to the mixture
10. Add the mixture to the zucchini boat and sprinkle with the parmesan
11. Place in a baking dish and bake for 35-45 minutes until the zucchini is tender and cheese is lightly browned

"Who knows what women can be when they are finally free to be themselves."
Betty Friedan

2-3 serves Chickpea Veggie Salad

Ingredients

2 cp	Spinach
2	Eggs, boiled
1/4 cp	Red onion, chopped
1/4 cp	Cucumbers
1/2 cp	Chickpeas
1/3 cp	Cherry tomatoes
	Blue cheese, to taste
1/4 cp	Balsamic vinaigrette
1/4 cp	Fat free honey mustard

Instructions

1 Add all ingredients into bowl

2 In a separate bowl combine the mustard and vinaigrette and pour on top

"We must believe that we are gifted for something, and that this thing, at whatever cost, must be attained"
Marie Curie

4-6 serves Lentil Soup

Ingredients

1/4 cp	Olive oil		1 cp	Brown lentils
1	Yellow onion, chopped		4 cp	Vegetable broth
2	Carrots, peeled and chopped		2 cp	Water
3	Garlic cloves, minced		1 tsp	Salt
2 tsp	Ground cumin			Red pepper flakes, pinch
1 tsp	Curry powder		1 cp	Collard greens or kale,
1/2 tsp	Dried thyme			chopped ribs removed
1 can	Diced tomatoes, drained			Half lemon, juiced

Instructions

1. Warm olive oil in a large dutch oven or pot with medium heat
2. Once the oil is simmering, add the chopped onion and carrot and cook, stirring often, until the onion has softened about 5 minutes
3. Add garlic, cumin, curry powder, and thyme
4. Stir for 30 seconds
5. Pour in the drained diced tomatoes and cook for a few more minutes, stirring often
6. Pour in the lentils, broth and water
7. Add 1 teaspoon salt and red pepper flakes
8. Raise heat and bring the mixture to a boil, then partially cover the pot and reduce heat to simmer
9. Cook for 30 minutes
10. Transfer 2 cups of the soup to the blender
11. Pour the pureed soup into the pot and add the chopped greens
12. Cook for 5 more minutes.
13. Remove pot from heat and stir in lemon juice

"No man is good enough to govern any woman without her consent"
Susan B. Anthony

10 serves Chicken Noodle Soup

Ingredients

1 tsp	Olive oil		1 pk	Tofu, extra firm cut into bit sized pieces
1	Yellow onions, chopped			
3	Garlic cloves, minced		2 qt	Vegetable broth
2	Carrots, sliced		6 oz	Dried wide egg noodles
2	Celery ribs, sliced			Salt and pepper, to taste
3	Fresh thyme sprigs			

Instructions

1 Heat oil in large dutch oven over medium heat

2 Add Onions, carrots, celery, garlic, and thyme

3 Cook and stir for 3 min; add tofu

4 Cook for 5 min or until vegetables are softened

5 Add broth and bring to boil

6 Once boiling, add noodles and simmer for 8 min.
   (if you plan to freeze the soup boil noodles in a separate pot so
   that the noodles don't get mushy)

7 Season with salt and pepper

Entrees

"I believe in the power of the voice of women"
Malala Yousafzai

3-4 serves Tofu Banh Mi Sandwiches

Ingredients

1 pk	Tofu, extra firm	1	*Daikon, sliced matchsticks
1/2 tbs	Olive oil, for the pan	2	*Carrots, sliced matchsticks
1	Baguette	1/2	*Cucumber, sliced into matchsticks
1 cp	Plain yogurt		
	Cilantro, to top the sandwich	1/2	*Jalapeno, thinly sliced
	Siracha, to taste	1/4 cp	*White wine vinegar
		1/4 cp	*Rice vinegar
			*Sugar, to taste
			*Salt, to taste

Tofu marinade

1 tbs	Olive oil
2 tbs	Soy sauce
1/2	Lime juice and zest
1	Garlic clove, minced
1 tsp	Ginger, minced

Pickled ingredients: Make ahead: Place thinly sliced daikon, carrots, cucumbers, and jalapenos in a jar with white wine vinegar, rice vinegar, sugar and salt. Liquids should cover veggies. Let chill for an hour to 1 week in the fridge.

Instructions

1. Drain tofu and slice into 1/2 inch strips. Dry to remove excess water.
2. Whisk olive oil, soy sauce, lime zest, garlic, ginger in bowl
3. Put tofu in a shallow pan and pour marinade on top
4. Let marinate for 15 minutes
5. Heat in a skillet to medium to high heat.
6. Add oil to the pan and cook for a few minutes on each side until golden brown and caramelized around the edges
7. Remove from heat
8. Assemble sandwiches with yogurt, tofu, pickled veggies, cilantro and serve with Siracha

"My mother told me two things constantly. One was to be a lady, and the other was to be independent"
Ruth Bader Ginsburg

4 Hot Chili Grilled Cheese

serves

Ingredients

4	Poblano peppers
1 can	Pinto beans, 14 oz can
3 tbs	Prepared salsa
1/8 tsp	Salt
1/2 cp	Cheddar cheese, shredded
2 tbs	Plain yogurt
3 tbs	Scallions, sliced
2 tbs	Fresh cilantro, chopped
8 slices	Sourdough bread, sliced

Instructions

1. Place peppers in microwave safe bowl, cover with plastic wrap and microwave 3-4 minutes until soft
2. Combine beans, salsa and salt in a medium bowl
3. Mash the beans with fork until they form a paste
4. Combine cheese, yogurt, scallions, and cilantro in a bowl
5. When the peppers are cool enough slice each one in half lengthwise and remove stem and seeds
6. Heat panini maker to high
7. Spread cup of bean mixture on each of the 4 slices of bread
8. Top with cheese mixture
9. Place two pepper halves and cover with bread

   * Note you can do this on the stove on a non stick skillet, recommended on panini press

"In politics if you want anything said, ask a man; if you want anything done, ask a woman"
Margaret Thatcher

2-3 serves Quinoa Black Bean Tacos

Ingredients

1 tbs	Olive oil
1 cp	Red onion, chopped
2	Garlic cloves, minced
3 tbs	Tomato paste
1 tsp	Ground cumin
1/2 tsp	Chili powder
1/2 cp	Quinoa

1 cp	Vegetable broth
1	Black beans rinsed & drained
	14 oz can
1/4 tsp	Salt
	Corn tortillas
	Pickled jalapenos
	Radishes
	Crumbled feta cheese

Avocado Sauce

1	Avocado, sliced into strips
2	Limes, juiced
1	Jalapeno, chopped
	Fresh cilantro, to taste
1/2 tsp	Salt

Instructions

1. Warm olive oil in a pot over medium heat
2. Saute the onion and garlic with a dash of salt for 4-5 minutes
3. Add the tomato paste, cumin and chili powder and saute for another minute
4. Add the quinoa and 1 cup broth. Bring the mixture to a boil, then cover the pot, reduce heat to a simmer and cook for 15 minutes
5. Remove quinoa from heat and let it rest still covered for 5 minutes
6. Uncover the pot, drain excess liquid and fluff with a fork
7. Stir in the drained black beans and add salt and pepper
8. Cover and set aside for a couple of min to warm up beans
9. Combine the ingredients as listed for sauce in a food processor or blender Blend well and season to taste
10. In a large skillet warm the tortillas
11. Assemble tacos with sauce on top with any other garnishes you would like to add

"You don't luck into integrity you work at it"
Betty White

4-6 serves Three Bean Chili

Ingredients

2 tsp	Olive oil	1	Green bell pepper, chopped
1 cp	Onion, chopped	2	Garlic cloves, minced
1 can	Garbanzo beans, rinsed and drained	3/4 cp	Water
1 can	Red kidney beans, rinsed and drained	2 tbs	Tomato paste
		2 tsp	Ground cumin
1 can	Black beans, rinsed and drained	1 tsp	Pepper
		1/4 cp	Cilantro
1 qt	Vegetable broth	1	Jalapeno
1 can	Diced tomatoes, undrained		Sour cream, optional
1 tbs	Yellow cornmeal		

Instructions

1 Heat olive oil.

2 Add onion, pepper, garlic and jalapeno to pan

3 Saute 3 minutes

4 Stir in 3/4 cup water, beans, tomato paste, chili powder, and cumin

5 Add cornmeal and cook 2 minutes

6 Remove from heat, add in cilantro and sour cream

"Where there is no struggle there is no strength"
Oprah Winfrey

4 serves Peanut Stew

Ingredients

1 tbs	Vegetable oil
4	Garlic cloves, minced
1 inch	Fresh grated ginger
1	Sweet potato, diced
1	Onion, chopped
1 tsp	Cumin
1/4 tsp	Crushed red pepper
1	Tomato paste, 6 oz can
1/2 cp	Chunky peanut butter
6 cp	Vegetable broth
1/2 bnch	Collard greens
1/4 bnch	Cilantro, for garnish

Instructions

1. Saute the ginger and garlic in vegetable oil over medium heat for 1-2 minutes
2. Dice the onion, add it to the pot, and continue to saute
3. Dice the sweet potato (1/2 inch cubes), add it to the pot, and continue to saute a few more minutes
4. Season with cumin and red pepper flakes
5. Add tomato paste and peanut butter, and stir
6. Add the vegetable broth and stir to dissolve the thick tomato paste peanut butter mixture
7. Place a lid on the pot and turn the heat on high
8. While the soup comes to a boil, prepare the collard greens
9. Remove the stems of the collard greens and cut them into strips
10. Once the soup reaches a boil, turn the heat down to low and let simmer without lid for 15 minutes
11. Once soft, smash about half of the sweet potatoes with the back of the wooden spoon to help thicken the soup
12. Serve with cilantro and salt to taste

"I call myself a feminist when people ask me if I am, and of course I am cause it's about equality..."
Ellen Page

6 serves Vegetable Mac & Cheese

Ingredients

1 lb	Plum tomatoes		2 cp	Sharp cheddar, grated
6 cp	Broccoli, florets		2 tbs	Dijon mustard
2 tsp	Olive oil		1 tsp	Salt
3 tbs	Butter		2 tsp	Pepper
3 tbs	All purpose flour		2 tbs	Fresh thyme, chopped
4 cp	Milk		1 lb	Penne
2 cp	Grated asiago			

Instructions

1 Heat oven to 400°
2 Slice tomatoes 1/4 inch thick
3 Coat tomatoes and broccoli with olive oil and roast separately on parchment lined baking pans for 10 minutes
4 Whisk butter and flour in a pot over medium heat until it foams
5 Add milk and whisk until thickened and bubbling, about 3 minutes
6 Remove from heat
7 Whisk in the cheeses, mustard, salt, pepper, and thyme
8 Stir in pasta and broccoli and transfer to a baking dish
9 Top with the tomatoes and bake 30 minutes

"Civilization is a method of living, an attitude of equal respect for all men."
Jane Addams

4 serves   Palak Dal

Ingredients

1 cp	Urad dal		2	Tomatoes, chopped
6 cp	Water (more if necessary)		1/2 tsp	Salt
1/2 lb	Spinach, finely chopped		2 tbs	Butter
1 tbs	Ginger, grated		1/2 tsp	Cumin seeds
1/2 tsp	Turmeric		1 tsp	Red chili powder
2	Green chili peppers, minced		1/2	Lemon juice
			1/4 cp	Cilantro, chopped

Instructions

1. In a large pot over medium heat combine the dal and water
2. Bring to a boil, then add the spinach, ginger, turmeric, 3/4 of the green chilies, and all of the tomatoes.
3. Reduce the heat, and simmer for 1 1/2 to 2 hours so that the lentils are soft. You may need to add some water during the cooking process
4. After and hour and a half, stir in the salt
5. In a separate pan, heat the butter and cumin and fry until the cumin seeds start to pop
6. Add the chili powder and fry for another 30 seconds
7. Add this butter mixture to the lentils and allow to cook for another 5 minutes
8. Taste, and season with more salt if needed
9. Top with cilantro and remaining green chilies

"It took me quite a long time to develop a voice, and now that I have it I am not going to be silent"

Madeleine Albright

3-4 serves Jackfruit Tostada

Ingredients

2	Young green jackfruit in brine, 2 20 oz cans	1/2 tsp	Smoked paprika
2 tbs	Chili powder	1/4 tsp	Cayenne pepper
1 tbs	Cumin	1	Onion
1 tbs	Oregano	4	Garlic cloves, minced
1 tsp	Pepper	12 oz	Salsa, of your choosing
		1	Lime, juiced
		1	Avocado sliced
			Tostadas

Instructions

1. Drain and rinse the jackfruit
2. Press moisture out of fruit and add to the crockpot or stove top pot
3. Season the jackfruit with the spices
4. Add the chopped onion and garlic to the crock pot and cover with salsa
5. Squeeze lime over everything, turn on the crock pot and let it go for anywhere between 3-8 hours stirring occasionally
6. When jackfruit is done it will be browned
7. Serve on the tostada, add avocado and any other preferred toppings

"I like my men the way I like my coffee, I don't drink coffee"
Ellen Degeneres

2-4 _{serves} General Tso's Tofu

Tofu

1 pk	Firm tofu, 12 oz
3 tbs	Soy sauce
1 tsp	Chili garlic sauce
3 tsp	Canola oil
1 tbs	Maple syrup
5 tbs	Cornstarch

Sauce

2 tsp	Canola oil
2 tsp	Cornstarch
2	Garlic cloves, minced
1 tbs	Ginger, minced
1 tbs	Rice vinegar
1/4 cp	Maple syrup
3 tbs	Soy sauce
1 tbs	Water

Stir Fry

1 tbs	Canola oil
1 bundle	Green onions, chopped
5	Chilies, dried
	Sesame seeds, for garnish

Instructions

1 Drain and dry tofu and cut into cubes
2 Chop green onions, garlic, and ginger
3 Prepare sauce by combining oil, cornstarch, minced garlic, minced ginger, rice vinegar, maple syrup, soy sauce, and water in a small mixing bowl and whisk thoroughly
4 Heat a large skillet over medium heat
5 Add tofu to shallow mixing bowl with soy sauce, chili garlic, oil, and maple syrup
6 Toss to combine and let rest for 2 minutes, stirring occasionally
7 Put tofu in a freezer bag and add cornstarch until it's coated
8 Cook tofu on all sides until golden brown and set aside
9 Put oil, chopped green onions, and dried chilies in a pan and saute for 2 minutes
10 Add sauce to the tofu and vegetables for 1-2 minutes
11 Serve with rice and broccoli

"I would say that each of us has only one thing to gain from the feminist movement: Our whole humanity"
Gloria Steinem

2-3 serves Bok Choy Tempeh Tacos

Tempah

1/2 cp	Vegetable broth		2 tsp	Dried basil
1/4 cp	Soy sauce		1 tsp	Cumin
2	Garlic clove, minced		1/2 tsp	Paprika
1 tbs	Balsamic vinegar		1 pk	Tempeh broken into small
1 tsp	Siracha sauce			chunks, 8 oz

Taco

3 bnchs	Bok choy
1/2	Red bell pepper, sliced
1	Carrot, grated
1 tbs	Sesame seeds
	Taco shells

Instructions

1. Marinate tempeh: Combine all of the liquid ingredients in a bowl, then add the broken up chunks of tempeh
2. Refrigerate for an hour
3. Heat a large shallow saucepan over medium heat for 1 minute
4. Add the tempeh along with its marinade with bell pepper and saute for 10 minutes
5. Once the liquid is mostly gone and the tempeh is tender, lower the heat to medium low and add the bok choy and carrots
6. Continue to saute until bok choy starts to wilt
7. Remove from heat and mix in sesame seeds
8. Assemble taco

"You may encounter many defeats but you must not be defeated"
Maya Angelou

6 serves Eggplant Lasagna

Ingredients

2	Eggplants, sliced lengthwise 3/4 inch thick (8 slices)	1 tbs	Thyme leaves
5 tbs	Olive oil	1	Whole milk ricotta cheese, 15 oz container
	Salt and pepper, to taste	3	Eggs
1 cp	Mushrooms, sliced	1 cp	Parmesan
2	Garlic cloves, minced	2 tbs	Oregano leaves
		1 can	Marinara sauce, preferred

Instructions

1 Preheat oven to 400°

2 Arrange sliced eggplant in a single layer on two sheet pans

3 Brush 3 tbs olive oil, salt and pepper on both sides

4 Roast eggplant until golden

5 Turn slices halfway through about 25 minutes

6 In a medium skillet add 2 tablespoons of oil and the sliced mushrooms

7 Saute for about 7 minutes

8 Add the minced garlic and chopped thyme and cook for another 2 minutes

9 Once the mushrooms are cooked remove and set to cool

10 In a bowl add the ricotta, eggs, 1/2 cup of parmesan, oregano, mushrooms, 2 teaspoons of salt and pepper

11 Mix well and brush baking dish with oil

12 Spread half of the marinara sauce on the bottom prepared baking dish

13 Lay 4 slices on top followed by ricotta mixture

14 Lay another 4 slices of eggplant and finish with marinara sauce

15 Top with the remaining 1/2 cup parmesan

16 Bake until golden brown at 350° for 30 minutes

"Stand up. Fight back. You have a voice. Use it!"

Pussy Riot

2-4 serves Portobello Pepper Melts

Ingredients

1 head	Broccoli, florets
1 tbs	Olive oil
	Salt and pepper, to taste
2 cp	Portobello mushrooms, sliced
2	Red bell peppers, sliced
1/4 cp	Plain yogurt
1	Garlic clove, minced
4 slices	Country bread
4 oz	Gouda cheese, grated

Instructions

1 Heat broiler

2 Take baking sheet lined with aluminum foil toss broccoli with oil; season with salt and pepper

3 Broil until broccoli begins to char 5 minutes

4 Add mushrooms and bell peppers to sheet, season with salt and pepper, and toss to combine

5 Broil 8 to 10 minutes

6 Set aside

7 In a small bowl combine plain yogurt and garlic, season with salt and pepper

8 Spread evenly on the bread, top with vegetables and top with cheese

9 Place on baking sheet, and broil until cheese is melts 2-4 minutes

"I am my own muse, I am the subject I know best. The subject I want to know better"
Frida Kahlo

4-5 serves Pesto Pasta

Ingredients

2 cp	Arugala leaves, stems removed		1 pk	Cherry tomatoes
1/2 cp	Walnuts, shelled		1/2 cp	Pine nuts
1 cp	Parmesan cheese		2 cp	Basil, stems removed
1 cp	Extra virgin olive oil			
2	Garlic cloves, minced			
1 tsp	Salt and pepper, to taste			
1/2	Lemon, squeezed			
	Wide flat egg noodles			

Instructions

1   Over medium heat, lightly brown the garlic for 5 minutes

2   Over medium heat toast the walnuts until for 3 minutes

3   In a food processor, combine the arugala, salt, walnuts, pine nuts, basil and all of the garlic

4   Pulse while drizzling olive oil

5   Remove the mixture from the processor and put into a bowl

6   Stir in the parmesan cheese, pepper and lemon

7   Cook pasta and after draining add pesto

8   Top with halved cherry tomatoes

"The more education a woman has, the wider the gap between men's and women's earning for the same work"
Sandra Day O'Connor

6 serves | Mushroom Risotto

Ingredients

6 cp	Vegetable broth, divided
3 tbs	Olive oil, divided
1 lb	Portobello mushrooms
1 lb	White mushrooms, sliced
2	Shallots, diced
1 1/2 cp	Arborio rice
1/2 cp	Dry white wine
	Salt and pepper, to taste

3 tbs	Chives, chopped
4 tbs	Butter, salted
1/3 cp	Parmesean, grated

Instructions

1. In a saucepan, warm the broth over low heat
2. Warm 2 tablespoons olive oil in a large saucepan over medium-high heat
3. Stir in the mushrooms, and cook until soft, about 3 minutes
4. Remove mushrooms and their liquid, and set aside
5. Add 1 tablespoon olive oil to skillet, and stir in the shallots
6. Cook 1 minute. Add rice, stirring to coat with oil, about 2 minutes
7. When the rice has taken on a pale, golden color, pour in wine, stirring constantly until the wine is fully absorbed
8. Add 1/2 cup broth to the rice, and stir until the broth is absorbed
9. Continue adding broth 1/2 cup at a time, stirring continuously, until the liquid is absorbed and the rice is al dente, about 15 to 20 minutes
10. Remove from heat, and stir in mushrooms with their liquid, butter, chives, and parmesan
11. Season with salt and pepper to taste

"*Trying to be a man is a waste of a woman*"
Coco Chanel

6 serves | Coconut Curry Tofu

Ingredients

2 bnchs	Green onions	1 lb	Tofu, firm small cubes
1 can	Coconut milk, 14 oz can	4	Plum tomatoes, chopped
1/4 cp	Soy		Yellow bell pepper, sliced
1/2 tsp	Brown sugar	1	Fresh mushrooms, chopped
1 1/2 tsp	Curry powder	4 oz	Fresh basil
1 tsp	Ginger, minced	1/4 cp	Bok choy, chopped
2 tsp	Chili paste	4 cp	Salt, to taste

Instructions

1. Finely chop green parts of green onions
2. In a large heavy skillet over medium heat, mix coconut milk,
3. 3 tablespoons soy sauce, brown sugar, curry powder, ginger, and chili paste
4. Bring to a boil
5. Stir tofu, tomatoes, yellow pepper, mushrooms, and finely chopped green onions into the skillet
6. Cover, and cook 5 minutes, stirring occasionally
7. Mix in basil and bok choy
8. Season with salt and remaining soy sauce
9. Continue cooking 5 minutes
10. Garnish with remaining green onion

"Sometimes I wonder if men and women really suit each other. Perhaps they should just be neighbors who visit now and then"
Katharine Hepburn

4 serves Butter Roasted Tomatoes

Ingredients

1	Tomatoes, 1 28 oz can diced	2 tbs	Olive oil
4 tbs	Butter	1	Butter beans, 1 15 oz can, drained
3/4 tsp	Salt		
1/4 tsp	Pepper	3/4 cp	Breadcrumbs
	Thyme, dash	1 cp	Quinoa, cooked
2	Garlic cloves, minced		
8 leaves	Kale, thinly sliced		

Instructions

1. Preheat to 375°
2. Cook quinoa, set aside
3. In baking pan add tomatoes, butter, 1/4 tsp salt, pepper, thyme, and garlic
4. Stir and place in oven and bake for 10 minutes, then pull out and disperse melted butter.
5. Place aluminum foil over the top and bake for another 20 minutes
6. Meanwhile, in a large pan heat and add 1 1/2 tbs olive oil
7. Add kale and 1/4 tsp salt
8. Cook for 8 minutes on medium heat adding a tablespoon or two of water if needed to make kale tender
9. Stir in remaining 1/4 teaspoon salt, kale, and beans
10. Add quinoa
11. Stir in the rest of the olive oil into breadcrumbs, top with gratin
12. Bake at 350° for another 8 minutes uncovered
13. Then broil for 2 minutes until top is golden brown

"If you stand for equality then you're a feminist..."
Emma Watson

4 serves Falafel

Ingredients

1 can	Chickpeas
2 tsp	Cumin
2 tbs	Coriander
2 tbs	Cilantro, chopped
1	Garlic cloves, minced
1	Green chili, seedless, finely chopped

1 cup	Greek yogurt
4	Pita breads, to serve
	Oil, (for frying)

Instructions

1. Mash the chickpeas or puree coarsely in a food processor
2. Mix with the cumin, coriander, garlic and chili
3. Season and divide into 24 pieces of equal size
4. Shape each piece into a ball
5. Heat a little oil in a frying pan and cook the balls for approximately 6 minutes each or until crisp and golden
6. Toast the pita breads and slit the tops
7. Fill with the falafel and spoon a little yogurt on top

"No one can make you feel inferior without your consent"
Eleanor Roosevelt

4-6 serves Chana Masala

Ingredients

1	Onion, chopped	1 tsp	Coriander powder
1 can	Tomato, diced 15 oz	1 tsp	Garam masala
1 inch	Ginger, peeled minced	1/2 tsp	Turmeric powder
4	Garlic cloves, minced		Salt, to taste
1	Green chili pepper, seeded and chopped	1 can	Chickpeas, 15 oz can fresh cilantro leaves, for garnish
3 tbs	Olive oil		Water, as need
1 tsp	Chili powder	1 tsp	Cliantro, fresh

Instructions

1. Grind onion, tomato, ginger, and chili pepper together into a paste with a blender or food processor
2. Heat olive oil in a large skillet over medium heat
3. Pour the paste into the skillet and cook until the oil begins to separate from the mixture and is golden brown in color, 2 to 3 minutes.
4. Season the mixture with chili powder, coriander powder, gram masala, turmeric, and salt; cook and stir 2 to 3 minutes
5. Stir enough water into the mixture to get a thick gravy; bring to a boil and stir chickpeas into the gravy
6. Reduce heat to medium and cook until the chickpeas are heated through, 5 to 7 minutes
7. Garnish with cilantro

"Accentuate the positives - medicate
the negatives"
Amy Sedaris

1 Black Bean Sliders

serves 1

Siracha sauce

Ingredients

3	Scallions
1/3 cup	Black beans
1	Portabello mushrooms
1/2 cp	Panko bread crumbs
1	Egg
2/3 cup	Spinach
	Pretzel bun slider

3 tbs	Siracha
1 cp	Greek yogurt
1/4 tsp	Salt
	Walnuts

Instructions

1   Begin by washing all of the vegetables and drying them with a paper towel

2   Run the beans through cold water, dry them, then place them in the mixing bowl

3   Cut the scallions by first removing the outer skin layer, then cut the sprout tip end and the bottom end

4   Finely chop the scallion and add to the mixing bowl

5   Dice the mushrooms finely

6   Add the mushrooms to the mixing bowl

7   Cut the tomato in slices and set it aside for now

8   Season the mix with chili powder, salt, and pepper to taste

9   Add butter or extra virgin olive oil to the pan and set it to medium heat

10   Add the egg, bread crumbs, and walnuts to the mixing bowl and begin mashing all of the ingredients until thick and pasty

11   Once ready, form three patties of equal size and place on the pan

12   Turn over after 23 minutes

13   Wait another 23 minutes and then place them on a plate

14   Cut the pretzel buns in half and add the tomato and spinach toppings and last the black bean patty

Desserts

"I believe that the rights of women and girls is the unfinished business of the 21st century"
Hillary Clinton

6 serves Banana Cupcake

Ingredients

3	Bananas, mashed
1 cp	Sugar
2	Eggs, beaten
3/4 cp	Vegetable oil
2 cp	All purpose flour
2 tsp	Baking soda
1 cp	Buttermilk
3 tbs	Chopped pecans
1 cp	Confectioners sugar

Frosting

2 1/2 cp	Confectioners sugar
2/3 cp	Dark brown sugar
12 tbs	Unsalted butter, softened
1/8 tsp	Salt
1/3 cp	Maple syrup
2 tsp	Vanilla Extract
4 oz	Cream cheese

Instructions

1. Preheat oven to 300°
2. Grease cupcake pan (serves 14)
3. Lightly beat bananas and white sugar together in a bowl until smooth; add eggs, one at a time
4. Beat in vegetable oil, 1 to 2 minutes
5. Stir in flour, baking soda, and buttermilk; mix well
6. Fold in pecans
7. Pour batter into the prepared cupcake pan
8. Bake in the preheated 20 to 30 minutes
9. Sprinkle cupcakes with confectioners' sugar

Frosting instructions

1. Combine confectioners' sugar, brown sugar, butter, and salt in the bowl of an electric mixer
2. Beat on medium-high speed 1 1/2 minutes.
3. While the mixer is on add maple syrup and vanilla extract
4. Increase speed to high and beat in cream cheese
5. Continue beating until fluffy
6. Refrigerate until ready to use

"You cannot shake hands with a closed fist"
Indira Gandhi

3-4 <small>serves</small> **Dark Chocolate Brownies**

Ingredients

4 oz	Unsweetened Chocolate, coarsely chopped		2	Eggs
6 tbs	Unsalted butter		1 tsp	Vanilla extract
2/3 cp	Flour		5 oz	Butterscotch chips
1/2 tsp	Baking powder			
1/4 tsp	Salt			
1 cp	Sugar			

Instructions

1. Preheat oven to 325°
2. Butter 8-inch square pan
3. Stir chocolate and butter in medium sized saucepan over low heat until smooth. Cool to room temperature
4. Combine flour, baking powder and salt in small bowl
5. Whisk together sugar, eggs and vanilla in medium bowl until mixture is thick (about 3 minutes)
6. Whisk in melted chocolate mixture, then flour mixture
7. Stir in butterscotch chips
8. Transfer to prepared pan
9. Bake for approximately 28 minutes
10. Transfer pan to wire rack; cool completely
11. Cut brownies into squares

"The worst thing that can happen for people who don't want women to be strong is that we help each other & become a force"
Sarah Silverman

6 serves **Creme Brule**

Ingredients

1 qt	Heavy cream
1	Vanilla bean, split lengthwise
6	Egg yolks
1/2 cp	Sugar
1/2 cp	Sugar for topping

Instructions

1. Preheat oven to 325°
2. In medium sauce pan combine cream and vanilla bean over medium heat, bring to a slow boil
3. Remove from heat and cover for 15 minutes
4. Remove and discard vanilla bean
5. In a medium bowl mix egg yolks and half cup sugar together until light
6. Stir in cream, a little at a time, stirring continually
7. Pour the liquid into 6 small ramekins
8. Place ramekins into a large cake or roasting pan, pour enough water into pan to come halfway up the sides of ramekins
9. Bake for 40-45 minutes
10. Cool and refrigerate for several hours to 3 days
11. When ready to serve, cover top with 1/2 cup sugar and use either broiler for 5 minutes or use blow torch to create crispy top
12. Allow creme brule to sit for 5 minutes before serving

"Be fearless. Have the courage to take risks.
Go where there are no guarantees"
Katie Couric

12 serves Chocolate Chip Cookies

Ingredients

1 stick	Unsalted butter, room temp
1/2 cp	Sugar
1/2 cp	Dark brown sugar
2	Eggs
1/2 tsp	Vanilla extract
1 cp	All-purpose flour
1/2 tsp	Baking soda
1/2 tsp	Salt
1	Chocolate chips, 6 oz bag
1 cp	Quick-cooking oats
1/2 cp	Walnuts or pecans, chopped

Instructions

1. Heat oven to 350°
2. Mix butter and sugar until pale yellow and smooth
3. Add eggs and vanilla extract, mix for another 5 minutes
4. Add dry ingredients in order mixing them together
5. Use an ice cream to form dough into small balls
6. Scoop all of the dough and chill on it on a quarter sheet pan in fridge for 30 minutes before baking
7. When ready to bake space them well on lightly greased parchment paper lined sheet pan
8. Bake 11-12 minutes, let cool before serving

"You'll never do a whole lot unless you're brave enough to try"
Dolly Parton

4 serves **Banana S'mores Ice Cream**

Ingredients

4	Bananas, ripe
1/2 cp	Chocolate chips
4	Graham crackers, crushed
1/2 cp	Mini marshmallows

Instructions

1 Slice bananas into thin coins

2 Spread out on a parchment paper-lined baking sheet and freeze for 2 hours, or until frozen

3 Blend bananas in a food processor (or a blender) until smooth

4 Fold in crushed graham crackers, marshmallows and chocolate chips, then transfer mixture to a loaf pan

5 Garnish with more graham crackers, marshmallows and chocolate chips, and freeze until solid, about 1-2 hours mor

"I'm basically a feminist. I believe women can do anything they decide to"
Grace Kelly

4 serves **Individual Pumpkin Pies**

Ingredients

3 cp	Ginger snaps, crushed	2 cp	Heavy cream
12 tbs	Butter, melted	8 oz	Cream cheese, softened
1	Pumpkin puree, 15 oz can		
3 tbs	Sugar		
1 tsp	Cinnamon		

Instructions

1 In a large bowl, mix ginger snap crumbs with melted butter until fully coated

2 In a small bowl, mix pumpkin puree with 1 tablespoon sugar and cinnamon

3 With mixer beat heavy cream until stiff peaks form

4 Fold in cream cheese and remaining two tablespoons sugar

5 Among four mugs, layer ginger snap crust, pumpkin, and cream, alternating until you reach the top of the mug

6 Garnish with ginger snaps

Drinks

"*Women and elephants never forget*"
Dorothy Parker

4-6 serves Thai Iced Tea

Ingredients

4 cp	Water		2	Cloves, whole
4	Black tea bags		1 cp	Half and half
3/4 cp	Granulated sugar			Ice
2	Star anise			
1	Green cardamom pod, smashed			

Instructions

1. Bring water to boil and add the tea bags, sugar, star anise, cardamom pod and cloves
2. Stir until all the sugar disolves
3. Gently boil tea for about 3 minutes
4. Remove from heat
5. Allow tea to steep for at least 30 minutes and allow it to cool
6. Remove the tea bags and spoon out the anise starts, cardamom pod and cloves. If tea is still warm, refrigerate until chilled
7. Fill glasses with ice and pour in Thai tea leaving enough room to fill in your half and half. For an 8 oz glass add about 2-3 tablespoons of half and half for a creamier flavor

"My mission is to create a world where we live in harmony with nature"
Jane Goodall

8 serves Horchata

Ingredients

1 cp	White long-grain rice, uncooked
5 cp	Water
1/2 cp	Milk
1/2 tbs	Vanilla extract
1/2 tbs	Ground cinnamon
2/3 cp	Sugar

Instructions

1 Pour the rice and water into the bowl of a blender; blend until the rice just begins to break up, about 1 minute

2 Let rice and water stand at room temperature for a minimum of 3 hours

3 Strain the rice water into a pitcher and discard the rice
Stir the milk, vanilla, cinnamon, and sugar into the rice water

4 Chill and stir before serving over ice

"Feminism is for everybody"
Bell Hooks

4-6 serves Lavender Lemonade

Ingredients

1 ice tray	Ice cubes
1/4 cp	Dried lavender
2 cp	Water, boiling
3/4 cp	Sugar
8	Lemons
5 cp	Water, cold

Instructions

1. Place ice cubes into a 2 quart pitcher
2. Place the lavender into a bowl, and pour boiling water over it
3. Allow to steep for about 10 minutes, then strain out the lavender and discard
4. Mix the sugar into the hot lavender water, then pour into the pitcher with the ice
5. Squeeze the juice from the lemons into the pitcher
6. Top off the pitcher with cold water, and stir

CPSIA information can be obtained
at www.ICGtesting.com
Printed in the USA
LVOW06s2001281117
557890LV00036B/473/P